The Five People You Meet in Heaven

Mitch Albom

STUDENT PACKET

NOTE:

The trade book edition of the novel used to prepare this guide is found in the Novel Units catalog and on the Novel Units website. Using other editions may have varied page references.

Please note: We have assigned Interest Levels based on our knowledge of the themes and ideas of the books included in the Novel Units sets, however, please assess the appropriateness of this novel or trade book for the age level and maturity of your students prior to reading with them. You know your students best!

ISBN 978-1-58130-854-9

Copyright infringement is a violation of Federal Law.

© 2020 by Novel Units, Inc., St. Louis, MO. All rights reserved. No part of this publication may be reproduced, translated, stored in a retrieval system, or transmitted in any way or by any means (electronic, mechanical, photocopying, recording, or otherwise) without prior written permission from Novel Units, Inc.

Reproduction of any part of this publication for an entire school or for a school system, by for-profit institutions and tutoring centers, or for commercial sale is strictly prohibited.

Novel Units is a registered trademark of Conn Education.

Printed in the United States of America.

To order, contact your local school supply store, or:

Toll-Free Fax: 877.716.7272
Phone: 888.650.4224
3901 Union Blvd., Suite 155
St. Louis, MO 63115

sales@novelunits.com

novelunits.com

Name _____

The Five People You Meet in Heaven
Activity #1 • Prereading

Getting the "Lay of the Land"

Directions: Prepare for reading by answering the following short-answer questions.

1. Who is the author?

   _____

2. What does the title suggest to you about the book?

   _____
   _____
   _____
   _____

3. When was the book first copyrighted?

   _____

4. How many pages are there in the book?

   _____

5. Thumb through the book. Read three pages—one from near the beginning, one from near the middle, and one from near the end. What predictions can you make about the book?

   _____
   _____
   _____
   _____

6. What does the cover suggest to you about the book?

   _____
   _____
   _____
   _____

Name _____

The Five People You Meet in Heaven
Activity #2 • Word Map
Use Before Reading

Directions: Complete the chart and discuss with a partner.

Word Connotation
positive _____
_____
_____
_____

Word Denotation
sky _____
_____
_____
_____

HEAVEN

Movies about Heaven
Heaven Can Wait _____
_____
_____
_____

Songs about Heaven
Heaven is a Place on Earth
_____
_____
_____

Name _____

The Five People You Meet in Heaven
Activity #3 • Vocabulary
Pages 1–51

craggy (2)	shingles (3)	solvent (5)	gravity (13)
hydraulic (15)	feign (23)	razed (27)	pristine (27)
gingerly (28)	kiosk (29)	conjoined (30)	perversion (30)
sweatshop (39)	silver nitrate (40)	commodity (41)	barker (42)
tawny (42)	burly (51)	carnage (51)	impotent (51)

Directions: The teacher will assign you one word from the list above. Turn to the page where the word appears in the novel and examine how it is used in context. Complete the word map for your word and share your results with the class.

Word Map

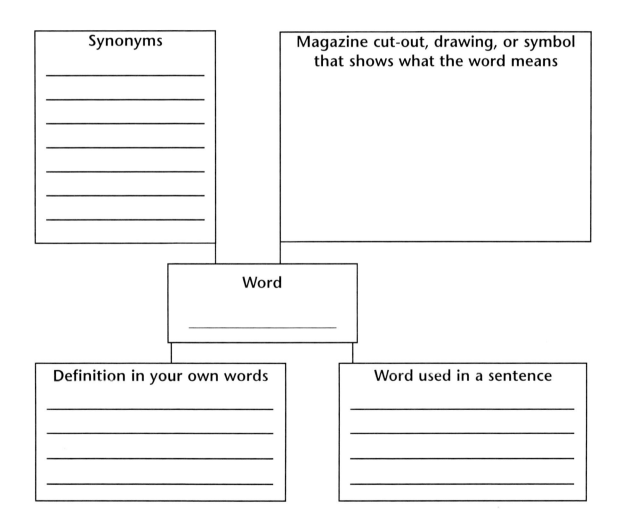

Name _____

The Five People You Meet in Heaven
Activity #4 • Vocabulary
Pages 52–97

seethes (53)	deflected (62)	bandoliers (62)	gaunt (67)
nubs (67)	promenade (78)	bile (83)	misshapen (85)
aspire (93)	murky (95)		

Directions: Use words from the vocabulary list to complete the following analogies.

1. ANIMALS are to ZOO as AMMUNITION is to _____.

2. SOUR is to LEMON as BITTER is to _____.

3. CALM is to RELAXES as AGITATED is to _____.

4. MONEY is to COINS as LUMPS are to _____.

5. VISUALIZE is to IMAGINE as DESIRE is to _____.

6. SHIFTED is to MOVED as TURNED is to _____.

7. PROACTIVE is to PASSIVE as BRIGHT is to _____.

8. CONFIDENT is to INSECURE as FAULTLESS is to _____.

9. BRILLIANT is to DULL as ROBUST is to _____.

10. ACT is to STAGE as WALK is to _____.

Name _____

The Five People You Meet in Heaven
Activity #5 • Vocabulary
Pages 98–144

firmament (98)	succulent (100)	oblivious (101)	gurney (102)
boardwalk (104)	veneer (106)	semaphore (108)	inexplicably (110)
abhorred (115)	incandescent (116)	roustabouts (121)	lathe (121)
pursed (133)	jetty (135)		

Crossword Puzzle

Directions: Select ten vocabulary words from above. Create a crossword puzzle answer key by filling in the grid below. Be sure to number the squares for each word. Blacken any spaces not used by the letters. Then, write clues to the crossword puzzle. Number the clues to match the numbers in the squares. The teacher will give each student a blank grid. Make a blank copy of your crossword puzzle for other students to answer. Exchange your clues with someone else and solve the blank puzzle s/he gives you. Check the completed puzzles with the answer keys.

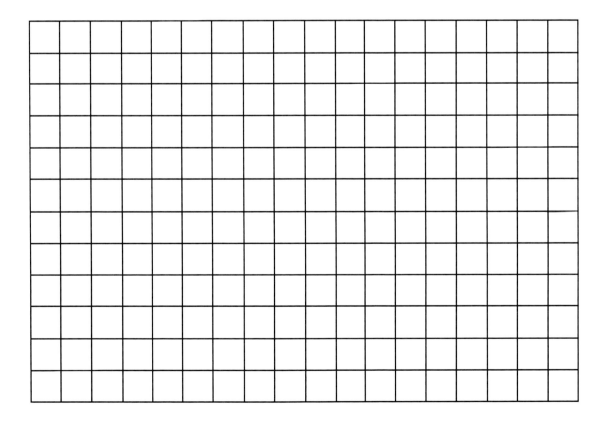

Name _____

The Five People You Meet in Heaven
Activity #6 • Vocabulary
Pages 145–196

lanky (147)	cadmium (151)	sheepishly (152)	tarantella (154)
flux (162)	flume (165)	protocol (167)	sallow (167)
wistfully (170)	portfolio (178)	cacophony (181)	iridescent (186)
plummet (188)	mottled (189)	mundane (193)	

Directions: Place each vocabulary word in the first column. Complete the chart.

Vocabulary Chart

Word	Part of Speech	Synonym	Antonym

Name _____

The Five People You Meet in Heaven
Study Guide

Directions: Answer the following questions on a separate sheet of paper. Starred questions indicate thought or opinion questions. Use your answers in class discussions, for writing assignments, and to review for tests.

Pages 1–18

1. Give the following information about Eddie: where he works, what job he does, how old he is. List four adjectives that describe him.
2. *Briefly summarize the last 50 minutes of Eddie's life in the following segments of minutes: 50, 40, 34, 30, 26, 19, 14, 12. Why do you think Albom gives a "countdown" of the last hour of Eddie's life?
3. *How do children react to Eddie? Why? What do they sometimes call him? What do you think the simile "They drew in like cold hands to a fire" (p. 3) means?
4. Identify Joe and Dominguez.
5. *Who is Marguerite? Where does Eddie meet her? Explain why you do or do not believe in "love at first sight."
6. What are Eddie's final words? How does he die?
7. Why is Eddie unable to stop the chain of events that lead to his death?
8. *What are the last sounds Eddie hears? Why do you think this is significant?
9. Who is Nicky? How does he inadvertently cause Eddie's death?
10. *Whose face is the last one Eddie sees on Earth? What is the last thing he feels? Do you think he saved the little girl's life?

Pages 19–36

1. *When is Eddie born? How does his father react? Why do you think this scene is important to the story?
2. What questions does Eddie ask himself immediately after his death?
3. *What does Eddie believe is missing after his death? Why do you think this is important?
4. *What does Eddie see as he drops toward the surface? What do you think this indicates?
5. What does Eddie's mother tell him about God on his fifth birthday? Why is this important to him?
6. What is the setting when Eddie awakens in heaven?
7. What are Eddie's first three thoughts?
8. *Describe Eddie's physical condition when he arrives in heaven. How does he react? What do you think this implies?
9. Where does Eddie meet the Blue Man? What does he initially tell Eddie?

Name _____

The Five People You Meet in Heaven
Study Guide
page 2

10. *In what stage of the Blue Man's heaven does he meet Eddie? What does he tell Eddie heaven is for? What do you think this foreshadows about Eddie's next stages of heaven?

11. How does the Blue Man explain Eddie's inability to speak?

12. *Prediction: How did Eddie cause the Blue Man's death?

Pages 37–51

1. Contrast Joe's and Eddie's reactions to the lost ball.

2. *Briefly describe the Blue Man's childhood and explain how you think this affects his life.

3. Why does the Blue Man's father quit speaking to him?

4. What causes the Blue Man to turn blue?

5. How does the Blue Man begin to work in the carnival? How does he feel about his work?

6. How does the Blue Man die? What role does Eddie play in his death? How does the Blue Man's death correlate with Eddie's eighth birthday?

7. Briefly describe Eddie's reaction to the Blue Man's story about his death.

8. *Explain what you think the Blue Man's statement, "Fairness does not govern life and death," (p. 48) means. Identify a time in your life when someone told you, "Life isn't fair."

9. Briefly explain the lesson the Blue Man teaches Eddie.

10. *What happens to the Blue Man as he prepares to leave? What do you think this symbolizes?

11. *How do people react at the scene of the Ruby Pier accident? What do you think they observe?

12. *Prediction: Who will Eddie meet next, and what will he discover about himself?

Pages 52–76

1. *Why do Eddie and Joe conflict on Eddie's 17th birthday? How is the conflict resolved? Explain whether or not you think sibling conflict is inevitable.

2. What is the setting for Eddie's next meeting in heaven?

3. *What causes Eddie to realize that "Fear had found him, even in heaven" (p. 57)? What do you think this symbolizes?

4. *What is Eddie's goal before enlisting in the army? Do you think he goes to war because he has to or because he wants to (see p. 60)?

5. Why does Eddie start going to the shooting arcade at Ruby Pier? How does Mickey Shea react to this? What does he tell Eddie about thinking?

Name _____

The Five People You Meet in Heaven
Study Guide
page 3

6. *Who does Eddie meet in this stage of heaven? What had been their association on Earth? What lesson do you think Eddie will learn from him?
7. State four things Eddie learns during the war.
8. What does the Captain promise his men?
9. Who is with Eddie when he is captured in the Philippines? What do they call their captors? Briefly explain the prison camp conditions.
10. Where are Eddie and the other captives forced to work?
11. *What causes Eddie to stop praying? Why do you think he makes this decision?
12. How do Eddie and the others escape? What do they decide to do with the prison after their escape?
13. *Prediction: What message does the Captain have for Eddie?

Pages 77–97

1. *What do you think is the most significant thing about Eddie's combination birthday/farewell party?
2. *Briefly describe the prisoners' furious act of revenge. What do you think this symbolizes to them?
3. What haunts Eddie about the hut he torches in the prison camp? What does he try to do?
4. What is the Captain's rationale for shooting Eddie, and what promise does he fulfill by shooting him? How does Eddie react when he learns who shot him?
5. *What effect does the leg injury have on Eddie? Explain what you think the statement "War had crawled inside of Eddie" (p. 85) means.
6. How does the Captain die?
7. What is the Captain's lesson for Eddie?
8. What has the Captain been waiting for before he can go to the next stage of his heaven?
9. *What changes does Eddie see in the landscape and the Captain before the Captain's departure? What do you think these changes symbolize?
10. *Prediction: Will Eddie ever learn whether or not he saved the little girl?

Pages 98–116

1. Briefly describe the setting for Eddie's next stage of heaven.
2. Who does Eddie recognize in the diner? How does this person respond?

Name _____

The Five People You Meet in Heaven
Study Guide
page 4

3. Where does the celebration for Eddie's 24th birthday take place? What is his physical and mental condition?

4. *Explain whether or not you agree with the statement, "All parents damage their children" (p. 104).

5. *What two types of damage does Eddie's father inflict on him when he is a child? Why do you think his father treats him as he does?

6. When he is a child, how does Eddie feel about his father?

7. Identify two occasions when Eddie's father shows pride in him.

8. How does Eddie's mother treat him when he is a child?

9. *How has Eddie changed after the war? How do you think this affects Marguerite, his mother, and his father?

10. *What leads to Eddie's final argument with his father? Explain the "final handprint on Eddie's glass" (p. 109).

11. Describe the third person Eddie meets in heaven. Briefly summarize her story and explain her significance to Eddie.

12. *What does Ruby tell Eddie about peace? What do you think this indicates about Eddie?

Pages 117–131

1. Briefly summarize Eddie's recurring nightmare. What effect does it have on him?

2. What causes the fire at Ruby Pier? What damage does it do? What is the result of this fire on Emile and Ruby? After the fire, how does Ruby feel about the pier?

3. *What information has Ruby come to tell Eddie about his father? Why do you think this is important?

4. Identify the illness that kills Eddie's father.

5. Name two changes in Eddie's life following his father's death. Why does he make these changes?

6. *Explain why you do or do not agree with the statement, "Parents rarely let go of their children, so children let go of them" (p. 126).

7. *What memento of his father does Eddie retrieve from his parents' apartment? Why do you think he chooses this?

8. Why does Eddie mentally curse his father for dying?

9. Who is Noel? Where do he and Eddie spend time together?

Name _____

The Five People You Meet in Heaven
Study Guide
page 5

Pages 132–144

1. What does Ruby remind Eddie was the result of his final verbal conflict with his father?
2. *Apply Ruby's statement, "Things are not always what they seem" (p. 137) to the information she reveals to Eddie about his father's death.
3. Why does Eddie's father save Mickey Shea's life? How does Eddie react to this information?
4. *What do you think Eddie's mother means when she keeps saying, "I should have done something…" (p. 139)?
5. *What does Eddie's father do just before he dies? What do you think this indicates about him?
6. For what has Eddie held his father responsible in the years since his death? What does Ruby tell Eddie he must do concerning his father?
7. Where in heaven has Ruby been waiting for Eddie? Why has she chosen this place?
8. *Explain the correlation between the statement, "Holding anger is a poison…hatred is a curved blade" (p. 141) and Eddie's third lesson in heaven.
9. *Where does Eddie see his father for the final time and what are his final words to him? What do you think this symbolizes?

Pages 145–159

1. Who pays for Eddie's funeral? According to Dominguez, what is Eddie's "unique quality"?
2. Where does Eddie's fourth stage of heaven begin? What is his physical condition?
3. *Where does Eddie meet Marguerite? What is revealed about their ages? Why do you think this is significant?
4. What kind of work does Joe do? How does his salary compare to Eddie's?
5. What surprise does Marguerite have for Eddie on his 38th birthday?
6. *Briefly explain why Eddie and Marguerite's marriage illustrates a "certain love" and how her death affects him.
7. How does Marguerite respond to Eddie's question about how much she knows since her death?
8. What does Eddie tell Marguerite about his death?
9. How does Eddie react to being with Marguerite again?

Name _____

The Five People You Meet in Heaven
Study Guide
page 6

Pages 160–175

1. Where does Eddie go on his 39th birthday? What happens there?
2. *Why does Marguerite start for the race track? What happens to her on the way? What role does "coincidence" play in this?
3. What effect does the accident have on Marguerite? on their plans for adoption? on Eddie?
4. *Explain how you think the simile "Love, like rain, can nourish from above" (p. 164) applies to Eddie and Marguerite's marriage.
5. *What eventually happens in their marriage? Why do you think this occurs?
6. What causes Marguerite's death?
7. What does Eddie tell Marguerite about Joe? his father? the war?
8. What does Eddie admit to Marguerite about his relationship with God?
9. Why is Eddie angry at Marguerite after her death?
10. Briefly explain Eddie's fourth lesson and how this correlates with Eddie and Marguerite.

Pages 176–196

1. *What does the estate attorney discover in Eddie's old box? What do you think this infers about his life?
2. *What does Eddie see after Marguerite leaves? What do you think this symbolizes?
3. Where does Eddie meet his fifth person? What is his physical condition?
4. *Why do you think Eddie's next birthdays are summarized so briefly? What does he do on his 82nd birthday?
5. Who is Tala? What does she tell Eddie? How does he react when he realizes her significance?
6. *What does Tala have Eddie do when she steps into the water? What happens as he does this? What do you think this symbolizes?
7. What is Eddie's fifth lesson?
8. What does Tala tell Eddie about the little girl whose life he tried to save? What is significant about the two hands he felt?
9. *Briefly explain your interpretation of the symbolism of Eddie's final arrival in heaven. Note the river, the pier, and where he meets Marguerite.
10. What is revealed about Nicky in the epilogue?
11. *Based on the final paragraph, what message do you think Albom wants to convey in his novel?

Name _____

The Five People You Meet in Heaven
Activity #7 • Literary Analysis
Use During and After Reading

Metaphors and Similes

A **metaphor** is a comparison between two unlike objects. For example, "he was a human tree." A **simile** is a comparison between two unlike objects that uses the words *like* or *as*. For example, "the color of her eyes was like the cloudless sky."

Directions: Complete the chart below by listing metaphors and similes from the novel, as well as the page numbers on which they are found. Identify metaphors with an "M" and similes with an "S." Translate the comparisons in your own words, and then list the objects being compared.

Metaphors/Similes	Ideas/Objects Being Compared
1. Translation:	
2. Translation:	
3. Translation:	

Name _____

The Five People You Meet in Heaven
Activity #8 • Character Analysis
Use During and After Reading

Character Analysis

Directions: Label the boxes below with the names of the following characters: Dominguez, the Blue Man, the Captain, Ruby, Tala, Mickey Shea, Amy or Annie, and the cumulative names of Smitty, Morton, and Rabozzo. Working in small groups, discuss these characters' attributes. In each character's box, write several words or phrases that describe him, her, or them.

Name _____

The Five People You Meet in Heaven
Activity #9 • Character Analysis
Use During and After Reading

Character Web

Directions: Complete the attribute web by filling in information about Eddie.

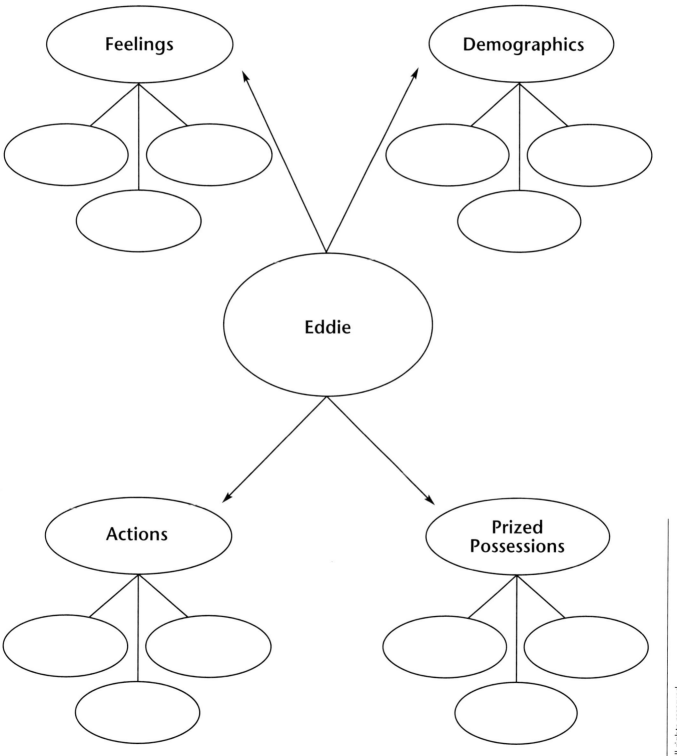

Name _____

The Five People You Meet in Heaven
Activity #10 • Character Analysis
Use During and After Reading

Sociogram

Directions: On the spokes surrounding each character's name, write several adjectives that describe that character. On the arrows joining one character to another, write a description of the relationship between the two characters. How does one character influence the other?

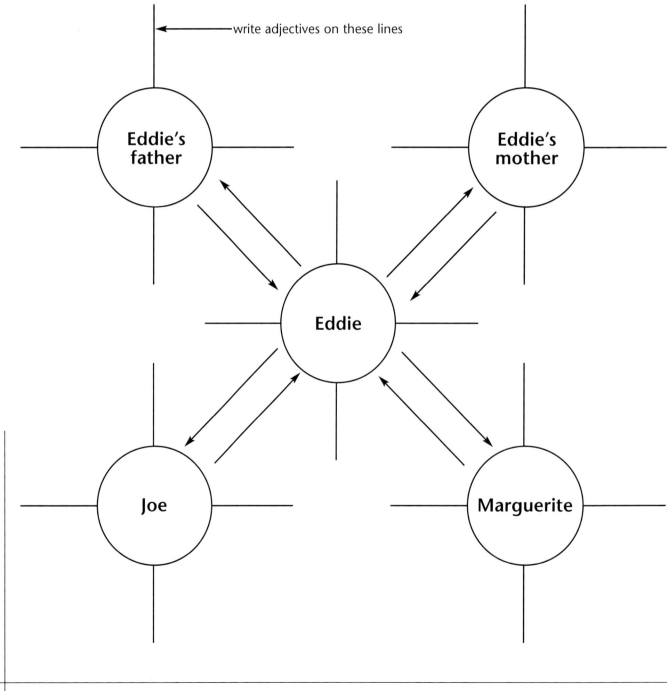

Name _____

The Five People You Meet in Heaven
Activity #11 • Comprehension
Use During and After Reading

Story Web

Directions: Place Eddie's name on a long spoke; on the short adjoining spokes write (1) his death (2) where it happens (3) why it happens. On the next five long spokes, place the names of each person Eddie meets in heaven; on the short spokes write the setting, the person's connection to Eddie, and his or her lesson for him. On the seventh long spoke, place Eddie's heaven; on the short spokes, write the setting, "Marguerite," and "Home."

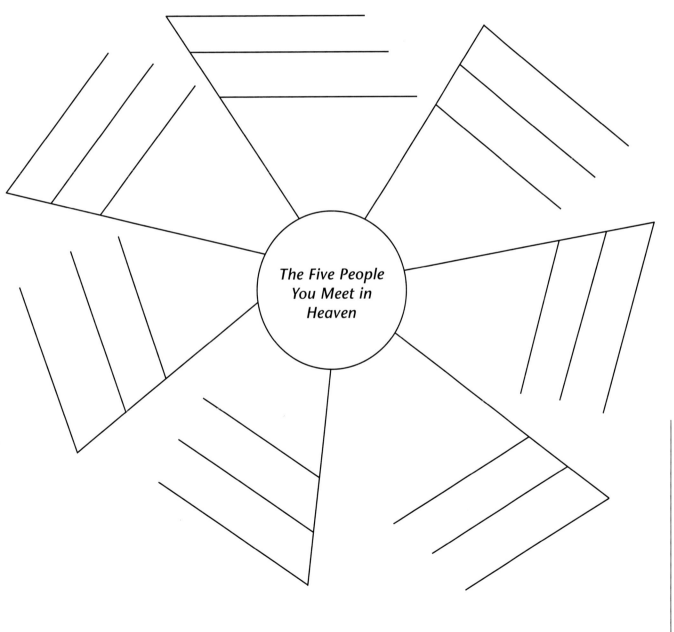

© Novel Units, Inc.

Name _____

The Five People You Meet in Heaven
Activity #12 • Comprehension
Use During and After Reading

Sequence

Directions: Sequence Eddie's life chronologically on the following diagram.

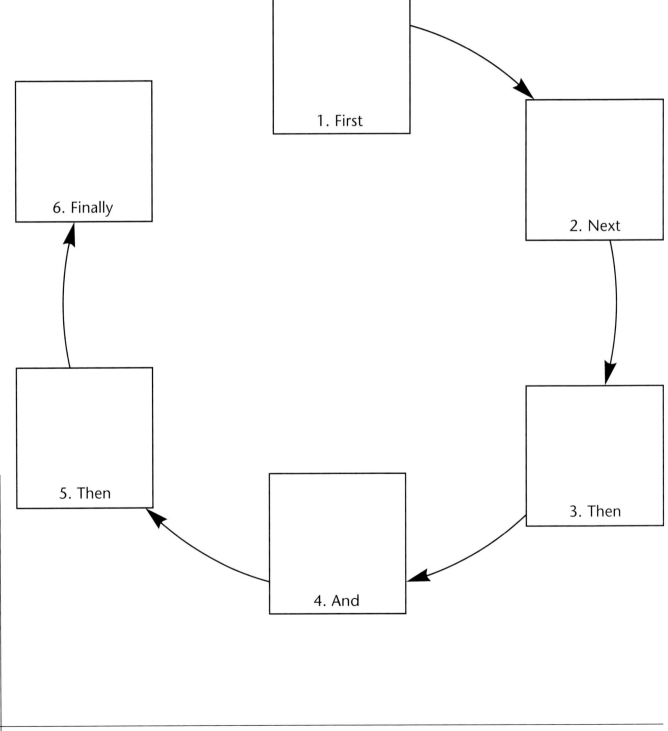

1. First
2. Next
3. Then
4. And
5. Then
6. Finally

Name _____

The Five People You Meet in Heaven
Activity #13 • Comprehension
Use During and After Reading

Conflict

The **conflict** of a story is the struggle between two people or two forces. There are three main types of conflict: person vs. person, person vs. nature or society, and person vs. self.

Directions: The characters in *The Five People You Meet in Heaven* encounter some conflicts in the story. In the chart below, list the names of three characters. In the space provided, list a conflict each character experiences. Then explain how the conflict is resolved.

Character:

Conflict	Resolution

Character:

Conflict	Resolution

Character:

Conflict	Resolution

Name _____

The Five People You Meet in Heaven
Activity #14 • Literary Analysis
Use After Reading

Thematic Analysis

Directions: Choose a theme from the book to be the focus of your word web. Complete the web and then answer the question in each starred box.

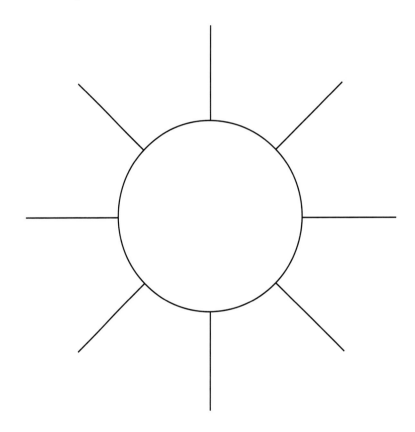

 What is the author's main message?

 What did you learn from the book?

Name _____

The Five People You Meet in Heaven
Activity #15 • Comprehension
Use After Reading

Fishbone Map

Directions: Choose a situation from the book that leads to a specific result. List the effect (result) in the box. Consider the causes. List causes 1, 2, 3, 4 (as appropriate). Add details to support the causes you list.

Cause # 1:
Cause # 2:
Cause # 3:
Cause # 4:

Detail:
Detail:
Detail:
Detail:

Result:

Name _____

The Five People You Meet in Heaven
Quiz #1
Pages 1–51

A. True/False

____ 1. All the customers at the amusement park like Eddie.

____ 2. Eddie first sees Marguerite in the halls of the high school.

____ 3. Eddie has often wanted to find a different job.

____ 4. Eddie is in great physical pain when he arrives at his first stage in heaven.

____ 5. The Blue Man was normal when he was born.

B. Short Answers: Answer each question in a complete sentence.

6. Where does Eddie spend the last hour of his life?
   _____

7. How does Eddie die?
   _____

8. Where is Eddie when he first awakens in heaven?
   _____

9. How is Eddie responsible for the Blue Man's death?
   _____

10. What is the Blue Man's lesson for Eddie?
    _____

C. Open-Ended Comprehension:
On the lines below, explain what the Blue Man's change in appearance might symbolize.

_____
_____
_____
_____
_____
_____
_____
_____

Name _____

The Five People You Meet in Heaven
Quiz #2
Pages 52–97

A. Fill in the Blanks

1. Eddie's brother's name is _____.
2. The setting for Eddie's meeting with the Captain is _____.
3. The Captain, Eddie, and other prisoners are forced to work in _____.
4. During the war, Eddie stops praying after _____.
5. Eddie uses his _____ skill to set up the prisoners' escape.
6. After their escape, the captives' rage causes them to _____.
7. Eddie tries to enter a burning hut because _____.
8. _____ shoots Eddie.
9. The Captain fulfills his vow to his men that _____.
10. The Captain's lesson for Eddie is _____.

B. Open-Ended Comprehension:
On the lines below, briefly explain what the Captain has been waiting for and the effect it has on him.

_____
_____
_____
_____
_____
_____
_____
_____

Name _____

The Five People You Meet in Heaven
Quiz #3
Pages 98–144

A. True/False

____ 1. In his third stage of heaven, Eddie sees many people in a diner.

____ 2. Eddie's father takes out his frustrations over losing card games by beating his sons.

____ 3. Eddie's father never displays any pride in Eddie.

____ 4. Eddie's father quits speaking to him because he objects to the war.

____ 5. Ruby tells Eddie he will never have peace until he makes it with himself.

____ 6. Emile builds Ruby Pier to commemorate where he and Ruby were married.

____ 7. Fireworks cause the fire at Ruby Pier.

____ 8. Ruby explains to Eddie why his father died.

____ 9. Mickey Shea deliberately causes the death of Eddie's father.

____ 10. Eddie's words, "It's fixed," indicate that Eddie has forgiven his father.

B. Open-Ended Comprehension: On the lines below, explain how Eddie's anger has poisoned his life.

_____
_____
_____
_____
_____
_____
_____
_____
_____
_____

Name _____

The Five People You Meet in Heaven
Quiz #4
Pages 145–196

A. Short Answers: Answer each question in a complete sentence.

1. Where is Marguerite going when she is severely injured in a car accident?
   _____

2. What is Marguerite's lesson for Eddie?
   _____

3. Name two things the estate attorney finds in Eddie's old box.
   _____

4. Where does Eddie meet Tala?
   _____

5. What does Tala tell Eddie about his job as maintenance man at Ruby Pier?
   _____

B. True/False

____ 6. The stage of heaven in which Eddie meets Marguerite features many weddings.

____ 7. Marguerite explains to Eddie how he died.

____ 8. Eddie and Marguerite never overcome the estrangement caused by her car accident.

____ 9. Eddie blames the war and his dad for his never leaving Ruby Pier.

____ 10. Marguerite waits for Eddie in a Ferris wheel cart.

C. Open-Ended Comprehension: On the lines below, explain what the items found in Eddie's old box reveal about him.

_____
_____
_____
_____
_____
_____
_____
_____

Name _____

The Five People You Meet in Heaven
Final Test, Level One

A. Identification: Match each character with the correct phrase.

___ 1. Eddie

___ 2. Ruby

___ 3. the Captain

___ 4. Marguerite

___ 5. Tala

___ 6. the Blue Man

___ 7. Eddie's father

___ 8. Eddie's mother

___ 9. Mickey Shea

___ 10. Joe

a. explains to Eddie how his father died

b. provides the tenderness in Eddie's childhood

c. tells Eddie there are no random acts and everyone is connected

d. makes three times Eddie's salary

e. tells Eddie he was destined to keep the children safe

f. inadvertently causes the death of Eddie's father

g. blames the war and his father for failure to achieve his goals

h. fulfills his vow to leave no one behind

i. is the harsh disciplinarian in Eddie's life

j. explains to Eddie that lost love is still love

B. Multiple Choice: Choose the BEST answer.

___ 11. Albom begins the novel with a(n)
    (a) new beginning for Eddie
    (b) description of Eddie's childhood
    (c) episode in the war
    (d) ending

___ 12. Eddie's physical description suggests all BUT which of the following?
    (a) his age
    (b) his agility
    (c) a war injury
    (d) the type of work he does

___ 13. During his last hour on Earth, Eddie
    (a) seeks spiritual counsel
    (b) repairs Freddy's Free Fall
    (c) goes about his normal routine
    (d) searches for a lost child

Name _____

The Five People You Meet in Heaven
Final Test, Level One
page 2

____ 14. Which of the following statements describes how Eddie feels about his job?
(a) It requires no more brains than washing a dish.
(b) He is proud to have followed in his father's footsteps.
(c) He believes his destiny has been to keep everyone who visits Ruby Pier safe.
(d) It requires a great deal of physical skill and mental expertise.

____ 15. Eddie dies because
(a) Dominguez fails to repair a ride properly
(b) he tries to save a child's life
(c) he is careless
(d) the crowd is unwilling to help him

____ 16. After Eddie's death, he wonders
(a) why he had to die
(b) what will happen to his estate
(c) where his pain and worry have gone
(d) why he doesn't see any angels

____ 17. The first stage of heaven Eddie enters is
(a) a war zone
(b) his childhood home
(c) a beautiful garden
(d) the Ruby Pier of his childhood

____ 18. The Blue Man explains to Eddie that people cannot speak when they first arrive in heaven because
(a) not talking helps them listen
(b) their vocal cords can't function in the thin atmosphere
(c) no one cares how they died
(d) they are babies who can't yet talk

____ 19. Eddie discovers that he inadvertently caused the Blue Man's death by
(a) failing to get medical help for him
(b) chasing a baseball into the street
(c) giving him silver nitrate
(d) running over him with a car

Name _____

The Five People You Meet in Heaven
Final Test, Level One
page 3

____ 20. When he goes to war, Eddie puts his dream of _____ on hold.
  (a) marriage
  (b) his job at Ruby Pier
  (c) becoming an engineer
  (d) graduating from high school

____ 21. During the war, Eddie stops praying
  (a) after the Captain dies
  (b) when he and his buddies are captured
  (c) after his leg injury
  (d) after Rabozzo is killed

____ 22. The prison camp conditions in the Philippines are best described as
  (a) humane
  (b) excellent
  (c) dismal
  (d) mediocre

____ 23. Eddie's ability to juggle provides
  (a) a way of escape
  (b) diversion from monotony
  (c) entertainment for the troops
  (d) a chance to join the circus

____ 24. Eddie staggers into the flames of a burning hut because he
  (a) wants to die
  (b) believes someone is inside
  (c) is trying to rescue Smitty
  (d) can't find the Captain

____ 25. The Captain shoots Eddie
  (a) because he is trying to escape
  (b) in order to save his life
  (c) because he blames him for Morton's death
  (d) so he can get a medal for heroism

Name _____

The Five People You Meet in Heaven
Final Test, Level One
page 4

____ 26. The Captain is free to progress to his next stage of heaven after he
   (a) receives Eddie's forgiveness
   (b) explains why he shot Eddie
   (c) explains the meaning of sacrifice
   (d) tells Eddie that he saved the child's life

____ 27. Eddie's father damages him in all BUT which of the following ways?
   (a) violence
   (b) silence
   (c) neglect
   (d) laziness

____ 28. Eddie and his father never speak again after
   (a) Eddie insists on going to war
   (b) his father beats him with a baseball bat
   (c) Eddie defends himself
   (d) his mother dies

____ 29. Eddie takes a full-time job at Ruby Pier because
   (a) he must look after his mother
   (b) he can't find another job
   (c) he wants to please his father
   (d) this is what he has always wanted to do

____ 30. Ruby's primary purpose in waiting for Eddie in heaven is to
   (a) tell him about his mother
   (b) help him find Marguerite
   (c) guide him to forgiveness of his father
   (d) explain why Emile built Ruby Pier

____ 31. As Eddie progresses through the stages of heaven, he becomes
   (a) stronger mentally and physically
   (b) more like an angel
   (c) mentally frail
   (d) physically weaker

Name _____

The Five People You Meet in Heaven
Final Test, Level One
page 5

____ 32. When Eddie meets Marguerite in heaven, she
   (a) looks as she did when she died
   (b) is a bridesmaid for a wedding
   (c) is waiting for him as his bride
   (d) greets him by a river

____ 33. Marguerite is injured in a car accident on the way to
   (a) find Eddie at the race track
   (b) meet Eddie to sign adoption papers
   (c) her job at Ruby Pier
   (d) tell Eddie of his father's death

____ 34. All BUT which of the following is a result of Marguerite's accident?
   (a) She and Eddie stop communicating.
   (b) The child they were going to adopt goes to someone else.
   (c) Eddie quits his job at Ruby Pier.
   (d) Eddie never gambles again.

____ 35. The pure, silent white Eddie encounters as he enters his final stage of heaven symbolizes
   (a) physical coldness
   (b) his inability to find the right path
   (c) his entry into purgatory
   (d) the isolation he feels after Marguerite leaves

____ 36. As Eddie washes Tala in the stream,
   (a) she tells him about her dream of coming to America
   (b) the other children join them
   (c) her singed flesh falls away
   (d) nothing changes

____ 37. Tala explains that Eddie saved Amy or Annie by
   (a) pulling her to safety
   (b) picking her up and throwing her off the track
   (c) covering her body with his
   (d) pushing her away from danger

Name _____

The Five People You Meet in Heaven
Final Test, Level One
page 6

___ 38. As Tala pulls Eddie through the river,
    (a) it cleanses him of the painful wounds and memories
    (b) he sees his father waiting for him
    (c) she tells him all about the war
    (d) he feels as if he is drowning

___ 39. "He (Eddie) was a leaf in the water" is an example of
    (a) simile
    (b) personification
    (c) allusion
    (d) metaphor

___ 40. "Her body is tossed like a doll" is an example of
    (a) irony
    (b) simile
    (c) metaphor
    (d) alliteration

C. Essay: Answer one of the following in a well-developed essay. Use specific examples from the novel to support your ideas.

(a) Explain how the theme of forgiveness is developed in the novel.

(b) Explain the lesson one person in heaven guides Eddie to understand.

(c) Explain the significance of Eddie's parting words to his father, "It's fixed."

Name _____

The Five People You Meet in Heaven
Final Test, Level Two

A. Identification: Complete the following charts.

Character	Setting in Heaven	Lesson for Eddie
1. Ruby		
2. Tala		
3. Marguerite		
4. the Captain		
5. the Blue Man		

Character	Primary Characteristic(s)	Importance in Eddie's Life
6. Eddie's father		
7. Eddie's mother		
8. Mickey Shea		
9. Amy or Annie		
10. Joe		

B. Multiple Choice: Choose the BEST answer.

____ 11. With which of the following statements does Albom introduce the meaning of the book?
　(a) "No man is an island."
　(b) "Love is the only thing that endures forever."
　(c) "All endings are also beginnings."
　(d) "No one can enter heaven unless he forgives those who have hurt him."

____ 12. At the beginning of the novel, Eddie's physical characteristics reveal all BUT which of the following?
　(a) his service in the armed forces
　(b) his childhood abuse
　(c) his job-related injuries
　(d) declining health

____ 13. During the countdown of the last hour of Eddie's life, he does all BUT which of the following?
　(a) takes two children on a roller coaster ride
　(b) gives Dominguez a gift of $40.00
　(c) makes a pipe cleaner dog for a little girl
　(d) goes for a maintenance ride on Freddy's Free Fall

Name _____

The Five People You Meet in Heaven
Final Test, Level Two
page 2

____ 14. The Blue Man's physical anomaly is directly related to
   (a) a difficult birth
   (b) his nervous disposition as a child
   (c) his desire to be different
   (d) alcoholism

____ 15. The dog tags hanging from a helmet sitting atop a rifle when Eddie arrives in his second stage of heaven symbolize
   (a) post-traumatic stress disorder
   (b) Rabozzo's death
   (c) the fear and death of war
   (d) Eddie's lost dreams

____ 16. All BUT which of the following occur while Eddie is a prisoner of war?
   (a) A guard kills Rabozzo.
   (b) The prisoners are forced to work in a coal mine.
   (c) Eddie intrigues the guards with his juggling skill.
   (d) Eddie burns down the entire camp.

____ 17. In the analogy comparing youth to glass and parents to handlers, the "final handprint" on Eddie's glass occurs
   (a) the first time he defends himself against his father
   (b) during the final beating he receives from his father
   (c) when his father rejects Marguerite
   (d) when his father objects to his going to war

____ 18. Eddie tells Ruby that heaven makes no sense to him because
   (a) he hasn't seen any angels
   (b) he has too many unanswered questions and no peace
   (c) his father won't speak to him
   (d) he can't find Marguerite

____ 19. Eddie resents his father for
   (a) never attending his ball games
   (b) the way he treats his mother
   (c) dying and trapping him in a life he hates
   (d) dying and leaving too many unpaid debts

Name _____

The Five People You Meet in Heaven
Final Test, Level Two
page 3

____ 20. The simile, "Love, like rain, can nourish from above...but sometimes must nourish from below" symbolizes
   (a) when Eddie first sees Marguerite
   (b) the gradual healing of Eddie and Marguerite's marriage
   (c) the death of their marriage
   (d) the healing power of words

____ 21. "Memory becomes your partner. You nurture it, hold it, dance with it" is an example of
   (a) irony
   (b) simile
   (c) allusion
   (d) personification

____ 22. Tala's purification in the river symbolizes
   (a) her restoration to Earthly life
   (b) a special medical treatment for burns
   (c) Eddie's understanding of his role on Earth
   (d) the cleansing of guilt and anguish from Eddie's soul

C. Open-Ended Comprehension: On the lines provided, describe Eddie's physical changes as he travels through the five stages of heaven, and explain what the changes symbolize.

_____
_____
_____
_____
_____

D. Essay: Answer one of the following in a well-developed essay. Use specific examples from the novel to support your ideas.

(a) Identify two incidences of "chance" in the novel and explain how these alter Eddie's life on Earth.

(b) Correlate the statement, "There are no random acts, and everyone is connected," to Eddie's journey through the five stages of heaven.

(c) Explain the father/son relationship between Eddie and his father and discuss how it affects Eddie's life as an adult.

Name _____

The Five People You Meet in Heaven
Alternative Assessment

Alternative Comprehension Assessment

Directions: Answer each question on the lines provided. Cite specific examples from the novel as evidence.

1. Explain the simile, "She (Marguerite) was like a wound beneath an old bandage, and he had grown more used to the bandage" (p. 10).

2. How does Eddie die? What does this reveal about him?

3. Where is Eddie when he first awakens in heaven? What does this symbolize?

4. What vow does the Captain make to his men in the Philippines? What must he do to ensure this vow is kept?

5. Identify Eddie's recurrent nightmare and tell what he discovers to be the source of this nightmare.

Name _____

The Five People You Meet in Heaven
Alternative Assessment
page 2

6. Explain what the Captain tells Eddie about sacrifice.

   _____
   _____
   _____
   _____

7. Explain the symbolism of the diner to Ruby.

   _____
   _____
   _____
   _____

8. Name three ways in which Eddie's father damages him.

   _____
   _____
   _____
   _____

9. Who tells Eddie "holding anger is a poison...hatred is a curved blade"? What do these metaphors mean?

   _____
   _____
   _____
   _____

10. Identify the setting of the stage of heaven in which Eddie is reunited with Marguerite and explain why this is significant.

    _____
    _____
    _____
    _____

Answer Key

Activities #1 & #2: Answers will vary.

Activity #3: Charts will vary. Example—Word: gravity; Synonyms: seriousness, solemnity, enormity, importance; Definition in own words: refers to the serious nature of something; Sentence: People need to consider the gravity of their words and actions.

Activity #4: 1. bandoliers 2. bile 3. seethes 4. nubs 5. aspire 6. deflected 7. murky 8. misshapen 9. gaunt 10. promenade

Activity #5: Answers will vary.

Activity #6: 1. lanky: adj., gangly, plump 2. cadmium: noun, chemical element, NA 3. sheepishly: adv., bashfully, boldly 4. tarantella: noun, folk dance, NA 5. flux: noun, change, stability 6. flume: noun, waterfall, quiet stream 7. protocol: noun, procedural rules, disorder 8. sallow: adj., pallid, rosy 9. wistfully: adv., longingly, contentedly 10. portfolio: noun, collection, NA 11. cacophony: noun, dissonance, harmony 12. iridescent: adj., shimmering, unchanging 13. plummet: verb, drop, climb 14. mottled: adj., blotched, unmarred 15. mundane: adj., ordinary, extraordinary

Study Guide

Pages 1–18: 1. Ruby Pier, head of maintenance, 83; white-haired, old, short, barrel chested, craggy faced (pp. 1–2) 2. 50: takes last walk along pier; 40: takes two little boys on roller coaster ride; 34: goes to maintenance shop; 30: gives Dominguez $40.00; 26: sends teenagers away from bumper cars; 19: sits for last time; 14: reminisces about Marguerite; 12: makes a pipe cleaner animal for Amy or Annie; Answers will vary (pp. 2–12). 3. like him; trust him; the ride man at Ruby Pier; Answers will vary (pp. 3, 5). 4. Joe: Eddie's brother; Dominguez: Eddie's coworker (pp. 4–5) 5. Eddie's wife; on the boardwalk at Ruby Pier; Answers will vary (p. 9). 6. "Get back"; when a falling cart strikes him as he tries to save a child's life (pp. 13–18) 7. Other workers can't hear him above the noise of the crowd (p. 17). 8. distant screaming, waves, music, rush of wind, his own scream; Answers will vary (p. 18). 9. a teenager who loses his car key on Freddy's Free Fall; the key wedges the pulley, causing the accident (pp. 10–11) 10. the little girl, Amy or Annie; two small hands in his own; Answers will vary (p. 18).

Pages 19–36: 1. 1920s; proudly smiles; Answers will vary (p. 19). 2. Where? What? Did I save her? Where is my pain? Answers will vary (pp. 20–21). 3. every hurt and every ache he's ever had; Answers will vary (p. 21). 4. sands of a golden shore; Answers will vary (p. 22). 5. God is proud of him for being a good boy on his birthday; the world seems right again (p. 25). 6. the Ruby Pier of his childhood (pp. 26–27) 7. He feels wonderful, he is all alone, and he is still on Ruby Pier (p. 27). 8. looks the same on the outside but has no pain and is limber; runs and jumps; Answers will vary (p. 28). 9. in the carnival sideshow; he has been waiting for him (pp. 30–31) 10. second; understanding his life on Earth; Answers will vary (pp. 34–35). 11. voice will come back; helps him listen (pp. 34–35) 12. Answers will vary.

Pages 37–51: 1. Joe trembles, cries, and runs away; Eddie grabs the ball and runs (pp. 37–38). 2. Polish immigrant, has to work in sweatshop with his father, suffers humiliation; Answers will vary (pp. 39–40). 3. because he is ashamed of him after other workers laugh at him when he soils his pants (p. 40) 4. takes too much silver nitrate for his nervous condition (pp. 40–41) 5. carnival men he meets in saloon ask him to join them; occasionally proud, thankful for the money (pp. 41–43) 6. has a heart attack; almost running over Eddie causes the attack; Eddie attends his funeral (pp. 43–44). 7. sorry, begs his forgiveness, says he didn't know (pp. 44, 47) 8. Answers will vary. 9. there are no random acts, all lives intersect, balance to everything, no life is a waste (pp. 48–50) 10. skin becomes lovely shade of caramel, smooth and unblemished; Answers will vary (p. 50). 11. with horror and shock; Answers will vary (p. 51). 12. Answers will vary.

Pages 52–76: 1. Joe teases him about Marguerite; mother gets them to dance with each other; Answers will vary (pp. 52–54). 2. war zone with fallen trees and blackened rubble (pp. 56–57) 3. sees his dog tags hanging on a helmet sitting atop a rifle dug into the ground; Answers will vary (p. 57). 4. save money to study engineering; goal is to build things; Answers will vary (p. 58). 5. has never fired an actual rifle and is going to war; tells him to shoot without hesitation; thinking gets you killed (pp. 58–60) 6. the Captain, his commanding officer when they served together in the army; fought and were captured in Philippines; Answers will vary (pp. 61–62). 7. to ride atop a tank, to be careful when shooting from a foxhole, to smoke, to march, to cross a rope bridge while carrying his gear, to pray quickly, to deal with death, etc. (pp. 62–63) 8. to leave no one behind (p. 64) 9. the Captain, Smitty, Morton, Rabozzo; Crazy One, Two, Three, Four; meager rations, filthy living conditions, harassment from guards (pp. 66–67) 10. coal mine (p. 69) 11. seeing a guard kill Rabozzo; Answers will vary (pp. 70–71). 12. As Eddie juggles for the guards, the captives take the rocks and strike the guards, eventually killing all four; burn it (pp. 72–76) 13. Answers will vary.

Pages 77–97: 1. Answers will vary. 2. torch entire camp with grenades and flame throwers; Answers will vary (pp. 80–81). 3. thinks he sees a small figure inside; go into the flames to help the person (pp. 82–83) 4. he would have died in the fire; not to leave anyone behind; screams, lunges for him, grabs him (pp. 84–88) 5. leaves him with a limp, believes it ruined his life; Answers will vary (p. 85). 6. blown up by a land mine as he scouts path ahead of the transport vehicle (pp. 89–90) 7. Sacrifice is a part of life (pp. 93–94). 8. Eddie's forgiveness (p. 94) 9. landscape transformed to pure, unspoiled beauty; captain clean, with pressed uniform; Answers will vary (p. 95). 10. Answers will vary.

Pages 98–116: 1. snowy, beautiful mountains with large lake in crest of two peaks; diner in a snowy field (pp. 98–99) 2. his father; remains oblivious to Eddie (pp. 100–101) 3. VA hospital; burns are bandaged, leg in a cast, depressed and wants to run away (pp. 102–103) 4. Answers will vary. 5. neglect and abuse; Answers will vary (pp. 105–106). 6. privately adores him (p. 106) 7. at a baseball game and when he wins a fight (pp. 106–107) 8. with tenderness (p. 104) 9. stays indoors, rarely speaks, stares out window for hours, won't get up and get a job; Answers will vary (p. 108). 10. Eddie defends himself when his father starts to strike him; Answers will vary (pp. 108–109). 11. old, gaunt, sagging cheeks, rose-colored lipstick, white hair, wears wire-rimmed glasses; poor as a child, meets wealthy man, Emile, while working in a diner and marries him; he builds Ruby Pier for her (pp. 110–116) 12. You have peace when you make it with yourself. Answers will vary (p. 113).

Pages 117–131: 1. He wanders through intense flames in the Philippines on his last night of the war, hears a constant squealing noise. Smitty yells for him to come on; something grabs his legs and pulls him under muddy earth; leaves him with feeling of darkness (pp. 117–118). 2. fireworks; completely destroys Ruby Pier; breaks Emile's spirit and his body; takes him three years to walk again; lose most of their money, move away, live modestly; wishes it had never been built (pp. 121–122) 3. why he died; Answers will vary (p. 124). 4. pneumonia (pp. 124–125) 5. takes a job as maintenance man at Ruby Pier; he and Marguerite move into an apartment in the building where he grew up; to look after his mother (pp. 127–128) 6. Answers will vary. 7. a deck of playing cards; Answers will vary (p. 127). 8. because he thinks it trapped him in the life he had tried to escape (p. 128) 9. a friend of Eddie's; at the horse race track (pp. 129–131)

Pages 132–144: 1. He picked himself up and started working (pp. 132–133). 2. Eddie understands that his father's pneumonia resulted from his saving the life of a friend and that Mickey Shea reacted to Eddie's mother as he did because he was drunk and depressed (pp. 133–138). 3. because of loyalty to a friend; can't understand why his father never said anything about it (pp. 137–139) 4. Answers will vary. 5. goes to the window of his hospital room and calls out for his wife, Eddie, and Joe; Answers will vary (pp. 139–140). 6. his abuse toward Eddie and Eddie's failure to achieve his dream; forgive his father (pp. 132, 141–142) 7. diner in the mountains; to have a place for all those who ever suffered at Ruby Pier to be safe and secure (p. 141) 8. His anger and hatred toward his father have poisoned his life and harmed him immeasurably (p. 141). 9. in the diner; "It's fixed"; symbolizes his forgiveness (pp. 143–144)

Pages 145–159: 1. Mr. Bullock, the park owner; He really loved his wife (p. 145). 2. wedding reception in yard of a home; back aches, leg is stiff, rotting away (pp. 146–147) 3. wedding in an Italian village; he is almost as old as when he died, she is young and beautiful; Answers will vary (pp. 149–150). 4. salesman for a hardware company; three times as much (p. 151) 5. a birthday cake and a group of children (pp. 152–153) 6. Their deep, quiet love sustains them through good times and bad times; devastates him (pp. 155–159) 7. knows everything that happened when they were together, that he loved her dearly, doesn't know how he died (p. 158) 8. The cart was dropping, and a little girl was sitting on the ride's metal base.0000. He tried to save her and felt her hands but doesn't know if he did so (pp. 158–159). 9. can hardly believe he's with her, hidden grief grabs his heart and overwhelms him (p. 159)

Pages 160–175: 1. horse race track; wins a great deal of money, then bets it all; argues with Marguerite by phone (pp. 160–161) 2. to find Eddie; has a car accident; A boy drops a liquor bottle over railing just as Marguerite's car passes under (pp. 162–163). 3. severely injured, requires bed rest for nearly six months; someone else gets the child; guilt drives him to lose himself in work and stop betting on horses; marriage suffers (pp. 164–165) 4. Answers will vary. 5. love and communication are finally restored; Answers will vary (pp. 165–166). 6. cancer (pp. 166–168) 7. died 10 years earlier from heart attack; has made things right with father; lost himself in war (pp. 169–171) 8. spent some of his time hiding from God, rest of time thinks God didn't notice him (p. 171) 9. She left too soon (p. 173). 10. Life has to end, but love doesn't. Eddie has never quit loving Marguerite and has never wanted anyone else (pp. 173–174).

Pages 176–196: 1. a black bow tie, a Chinese restaurant menu, a deck of cards, a letter with an army medal, picture of Eddie on his 38th birthday; Answers will vary (p. 177). 2. nothing but white; symbolizes his sorrow and isolation (p. 179) 3. by a river; aged as at his death (pp. 180–182) 4. Answers will vary; visits the cemetery (pp. 183–184) 5. the Filipino child Eddie saw in the burning hut; he burned her; deep sorrow and anguish, begs for forgiveness (pp. 185–189) 6. wash her with a stone; her singed flesh falls away; Answers will vary (pp. 189–190). 7. He was destined to maintain the rides to keep the children safe (p. 191). 8. He pushed her out of the way; They are Tala's as she pulls him to heaven (p. 192). 9. Answers will vary. 10. He is Ruby's great-grandson (p. 196). 11. Everyone's story is connected in some way (p. 196).

Note: Responses to Activities #7–#15 will vary, but the following are suggested responses.

Activity #7: Metaphors and similes are found throughout the book.

Activity #8: Dominguez: hard worker, respects Eddie, assumes Eddie's job; the Blue Man: sideshow "freak," humiliating childhood, caring, kind; the Captain: strict commanding officer, concerned, willing to sacrifice life for others; Ruby: poor girl who marries a rich man, wishes Ruby Pier had never been built, helps Eddie learn to forgive his father; Tala: five-year-old Filipino child, lovely, forgiving; Mickey Shea: alcoholic, depressed, never forgives himself for death of Eddie's father; Amy or Annie: child whose life Eddie saves, friendly, often alone; Smitty, Morton, Rabozzo: Eddie's co-prisoners of war, good soldiers, filled with rage over captivity, loyal

Activity #9: Eddie: Feelings—ineffective, angry, lonely; Demographics—maintenance worker, Marguerite's husband, son of abusive father; Actions—works hard, bets on horses, tries to save child's life; Prized Possessions—picture, menu, black bow tie, deck of cards

Activity #10: Eddie: short, muscular, active; Eddie's father: harsh, domineering, abusive; relationship with Eddie—controlling, unbending; Eddie blames him for dying and keeping him locked in an unfulfilling job; Eddie's mother: loving, tender, unable to cope with husband's death; she loves Eddie and at times tries to stop his father's abuse; Eddie looks to her for love and cares for her after his father's death; Joe: weak, proud, flashy; resents Eddie as a child, brags to him as an adult; Eddie resents his good job and money; Marguerite: beautiful, loving, gentle; loves Eddie more than anyone; Eddie returns the love and misses her acutely after her death.

Activity #11: Eddie: his death, at Ruby Pier, trying to save a child's life; the Blue Man: Ruby Pier, Eddie inadvertently causes his death, no random acts and everyone is connected; the Captain: war zone in Philippines, his commanding officer, sacrifice is a part of life; Ruby: diner in the mountains, her husband built Ruby Pier, things are not as they seem and Eddie must forgive his father; Marguerite: various weddings, his wife, lost love is still love; Tala: a river, child he had seen in burning hut, his job to keep children safe was destined to be

Activity #12: born in 1920s, grows up with abusive father, fights in the Philippines, marries Marguerite, takes job at Ruby Pier after father's death, dies saving child's life

Activity #13: (1) Eddie—Conflict: hates his father for abuse, neglect, and dying; Resolution: understands and forgives his father (2) Marguerite—Conflict: Eddie's gambling leads inadvertently to her injuries and loss of chance to adopt a child; Resolution: Their love eventually revives. (3) Eddie and other soldiers—Conflict: taken as prisoners of war; Resolution: kill their guards and escape

Activity #14: Theme: love; effect of lack of love on the Blue Man, Eddie's private love for his father, his father's expressed love in final moments of life, mutual love between Eddie and Marguerite, sacrificial love of the Captain, love lasts after death, Marguerite's love for children, mutual love between Ruby and Emile

Activity #15: Result: Eddie feels his life is ineffective and unfulfilling. Cause #1: gives up his dream of becoming an engineer, goes to war; Cause #2: his war injury, leaves him depressed and crippled; Cause #3: his father dies, he takes over his job and the care of his mother; Cause #4: Eddie loses his motivation, Marguerite dies

Quiz #1: A. 1. F (p. 3) 2. F (p. 9) 3. T (p. 5) 4. F (p. 32) 5. T (p. 40) **B.** 6. Ruby Pier (p. 1) 7. cart falls on him as he tries to save child's life (pp. 17–18) 8. back at Ruby Pier (pp. 26–27) 9. accident caused by Eddie chasing a ball into the street causes Blue Man to have a heart attack (pp. 29–30) 10. no random acts; all lives are connected (p. 48) **C.** Answers will vary. Refer to the scoring rubric on page 44 of this guide.

Quiz #2: A. 1. Joe (p. 52) 2. the war zone in Philippines (pp. 57, 61–62) 3. a coal mine (pp. 66–67) 4. Rabozzo is killed (pp. 70–71) 5. juggling (pp. 72–75) 6. burn everything in the camp (pp. 75–80) 7. he thinks he sees a small figure inside (pp. 81–83) 8. The Captain (p. 86) 9. he will not leave anyone behind (pp. 86–88, 94) 10. sacrifice is a part of life (pp. 93–94) **B.** Answers will vary. Refer to the scoring rubric on page 44 of this guide.

Quiz #3: A. 1. T (pp. 99–100) 2. T (p. 105) 3. F (p. 106) 4. F (pp. 108–109) 5. T (p. 113) 6. F (p. 115) 7. T (p. 121) 8. T (p. 124) 9. F (p. 138) 10. T (pp. 143–144) **B.** Answers will vary. Refer to the scoring rubric on page 44 of this guide.

Quiz #4: A. 1. to find Eddie at the race track (pp. 162–163) 2. Lost love is still love (p. 173). 3. black bow tie, menu from Chinese restaurant, picture of Eddie on his 38th birthday, deck of cards (p. 177) 4. bank of a river (pp. 180–181) 5. that's what he was supposed to do, to keep the children safe (p. 191) **B.** 6. T (pp. 147–150) 7. F (p. 158) 8. F (pp. 164–165) 9. T (p. 170) 10. T (p. 194) **C.** Answers will vary. Refer to the scoring rubric on page 44 of this guide.

Final Test, Level One: A. 1. g 2. a 3. h 4. j 5. e 6. c 7. i 8. b 9. f 10. d **B.** 11. d (p. 1) 12. b (p. 2) 13. c (pp. 2–12) 14. a (p. 5) 15. b (pp. 17–18) 16. c (p. 21) 17. d (pp. 26–27) 18. a (p. 35)

19. b (pp. 42–44) 20. c (p. 58) 21. d (pp. 70–71) 22. c (pp. 66–69) 23. a (pp. 72–75) 24. b (pp. 81–83) 25. b (p. 87) 26. a (p. 94) 27. d (pp. 104–109) 28. c (p. 109) 29. a (pp. 126–128) 30. c (pp. 141–142) 31. d (throughout) 32. b (p. 150) 33. a (pp. 162–163) 34. c (pp. 164–165) 35. d (p. 179) 36. c (p. 190) 37. d (p. 192) 38. a (pp. 192–193) 39. d (p. 193) 40. b (p. 163) **C.** Answers will vary. Refer to the scoring rubric on page 44 of this guide.

Final Test, Level Two: A. 1. diner in mountains; things are not always what they seem and he must forgive his father 2. river; his job as maintenance man was his destiny so he could keep children safe 3. series of weddings; lost love is still love 4. war zone in Philippines; sacrifice is part of life 5. Ruby Pier; there are no random acts, and everyone is connected 6. domineering, abusive; Eddie blames him for dying and keeping him in a job he hates 7. tender, loving; provides the tenderness Eddie needs 8. alcoholic, depressed; inadvertently causes death of Eddie's father 9. young, often alone; child for whom Eddie gives his life 10. fancy, vain; Eddie's brother who makes more money than he **B.** 11. c (p. 1) 12. b (p. 2) 13. d (pp. 2–11) 14. b (pp. 39–40) 15. c (p. 57) 16. d (pp. 68–76, 80) 17. a (p. 109) 18. b (p. 112) 19. c (p. 128) 20. b (pp. 164–165) 21. d (p. 173) 22. d (p. 190) **C.** Suggested response: He is young and pain free at the beginning but becomes progressively older and more feeble; loses all pain and weariness as Tala pulls him through the river to meet Marguerite; symbolizes redemption and new life. **D.** Answers will vary. Refer to the scoring rubric on page 44 of this guide.

Alternative Assessment: 1. The pain of Marguerite's death is like a wound he has covered (p. 10). 2. struck by falling cart while trying to save child's life; Answers will vary (pp. 17–18). 3. Ruby Pier; back where he started (pp. 26–27) 4. not to leave anyone behind; shoot Eddie in the leg (pp. 86–88) 5. He is in the village during the war, hears a squealing noise, something grabs his leg and pulls him down; Tala was in the burning hut (pp. 117–118, 187–188). 6. It is a part of life (p. 93). 7. a return to her younger years and secure life; wants a place of safety and security for everyone who ever suffered at Ruby Pier (p. 141) 8. neglect, violence, silence (pp. 104–109) 9. Ruby; anger and hatred destroy the person who holds those feelings (p. 141) 10. a series of weddings; symbolize their undying love (pp. 147–150)

Linking Novel Units® Student Packets to National and State Reading Assessments

During the past several years, an increasing number of students have faced some form of state-mandated competency testing in reading. Many states now administer state-developed assessments to measure the skills and knowledge emphasized in their particular reading curriculum. This Novel Units® guide includes open-ended comprehension questions that correlate with state-mandated reading assessments. The rubric below provides important information for evaluating responses to open-ended comprehension questions. Teachers may also use scoring rubrics provided for their own state's competency test.

Scoring Rubric for Open-Ended Items

3-Exemplary	Thorough, complete ideas/information Clear organization throughout Logical reasoning/conclusions Thorough understanding of reading task Accurate, complete response
2-Sufficient	Many relevant ideas/pieces of information Clear organization throughout most of response Minor problems in logical reasoning/conclusions General understanding of reading task Generally accurate and complete response
1-Partially Sufficient	Minimally relevant ideas/information Obvious gaps in organization Obvious problems in logical reasoning/conclusions Minimal understanding of reading task Inaccuracies/incomplete response
0-Insufficient	Irrelevant ideas/information No coherent organization Major problems in logical reasoning/conclusions Little or no understanding of reading task Generally inaccurate/incomplete response